Basic Instructions for Cutting, Sewing, Layering,
Quilting and Binding are on pages 12 - 15.

TIPS: As a Guide for Yardage:
Each $1/4$ yard or a 'Fat Quarter' equals 3 strips.
A pre-cut 'Jelly Roll' strip is 2½" x 44".
Cut 'Fat Quarter' and yardage strips to 2½" x 20".
Yardage is given for using either
'Jelly Roll' strips or fabric yardage.

Heart & Home
Quilt of the Month

pieced by Donna Hansen
quilted by Susan Corbett

*Heartfelt sentiments are included in every block
of this beautiful quilt. It reminds me of my favorite
times at home, with family, and in the garden.*

Heart & Home
Quilt of the Month

SIZE: 50" x 68"

Yardage
We used *Moda* "Madeira" by Blackbird Designs 'Jelly Roll' collection of 2¹/₂" fabric strips
- we purchased 1 'Jelly Roll'

6 strips	OR	¹/₂ yard Brown
5 strips	OR	¹/₂ yard Red
4 strips	OR	¹/₂ yard Teal
6 strips	OR	¹/₂ yard Green
19 strips	OR	1¹/₂ yards Ivory

Border	Purchase 1³/₄ yards Teal
Binding	Purchase ¹/₂ yard
Backing	Purchase 3 yards
Batting	Purchase 58" x 76"

Sewing machine, needle, thread

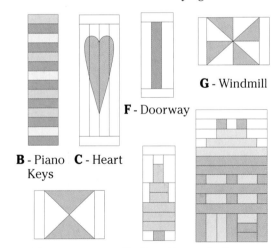

A - Flower Basket   **E** - Playing the Piano

G - Windmill

F - Doorway

B - Piano Keys   **C** - Heart

D - Hourglass   **H** - Pine Tree   **I** - House

Make and Sew the Blocks

Caution:
 Cut carefully.
 You will use ALL the strips.
 Cut the longest strips first.
See details for blocks on pages 6 - 11.

For each block, sew strips together in numerical sequence, pressing after each joining seam.
 1 to 2. Press.
 1/2 to 3. Press.
 1/2/3 to 4. Press.
 1/2/3/4 to 5. Press
 - and so on until the block in complete.

Label each constructed block the with letter and name.

Assembly

Arrange Blocks, refer to quilt diagram for placement.

Sew blocks together as follows:
Unit 1
 Sew Block B to C.
 Block A to B/C to D
Unit 2
 Block G to I
 Block F to H
 Block G/I to F/H
 Block E to F/H/G/I

Sew Unit 1 to Unit 2

Borders

Teal and Green Pieced Border
Choose 2 Teal strips and 3 Green strips.
Cut each strip into assorted lengths - varying from x" to x"

Randomly sew all Teal and Green pieces together, end to end.
 Cut 2 strips 2¹/₂" x 34¹/₂" for top and bottom.
 Cut 2 strips 2¹/₂" x 56¹/₂" for sides.

Sew top and bottom border to the quilt. Press.
Sew side borders to the quilt. Press.

Ivory Pieced Border
Choose 5 Ivory strips.
Cut each strip into assorted lengths - varying from x" to x"

Randomly sew all pieces together end to end.
 Cut 2 strips 2¹/₂" x 38¹/₂" for top and bottom.
 Cut 2 strips 2¹/₂" x 60¹/₂" for sides.

Sew top and bottom border to the quilt. Press.
Sew side borders to the quilt. Press.

Teal Outer Border
Cut 2 strips 4¹/₂" x 60¹/₂" for sides.
Cut 2 strips 4¹/₂" x 50¹/₂" for top and bottom.

Sew side borders to the quilt. Press.
Sew top and bottom border to the quilt. Press.

Finishing

Backing
Piece 2³/₄ yards to 48" x 64".

Quilting: See Basic Instructions on page 14.

Binding: Cut 2¹/₂" strips.
 Sew the strips together end to end to equal 244".
 See Basic Instructions on page 15.

Heart & Home - Quilt Assembly

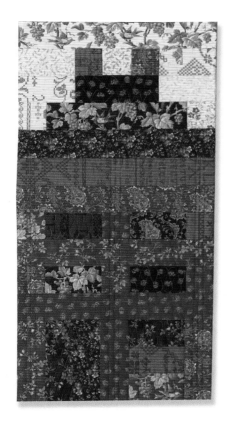

I - House Block

H - Pine Tree Block

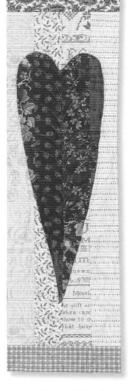

C - Heart Block

F - Doorway Block

A - Flower Basket Block

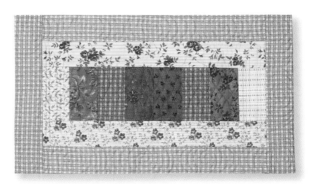

E - Playing the Piano Block

B - Piano Keys Block

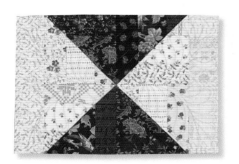

D - Hourglass

use Ivory &
Green

G - Windmill Block

use Gold & Brown

What You'll Need:

We used *Moda* "Madeira"
'Jelly Roll' collection of 2½" fabric strips
- we purchased 1 'Jelly Roll'

6 strips	OR	½ yard Brown
5 strips	OR	½ yard Red
4 strips	OR	½ yard Teal
6 strips	OR	½ yard Green
19 strips	OR	1½ yards Ivory

Border	Purchase 1¾ yards Teal
Binding	Purchase ½ yard
Backing	Purchase 3 yards
Batting	Purchase 48" x 64"

Sewing machine, needle, thread

Heart & Home

Sew a block a day, or make a block every week. Your quilt will be completed quickly.

These beautiful blocks are simple to construct and are really versatile. Put them all together in a fabulous quilt, or add extra border strips around the edges to make a pillow top or totebag.

Be creative with your colors. Since there are only 5 basic colors... Brown, Red, Green, Teal and Ivory... it is easy to make the quilt in your choice of fabrics.

Enjoy quilting.

I - House Block (diagram)

35

1	2	3	4	5
6		7		8
9		10		11
12
13
14
15	16	17	18	19
20
21	22	23	24	25
26
27	28	29	30	31 / 32 / 33	34

I - House Block

TIP: I like to cut and sew my most important blocks first. By doing this I can choose and use the best colors where I really want them.

Then, closer to the end, it is easy to substitute or use the less important colors and fabrics.

Preparation for Blocks

TIP: To avoid confusion, gather the strips for each block as you cut them and label by piece number.

All strips are $2^1/2$" wide by the indicated length.

Cutting Lists and Chart:s

The chart for each color includes:
Cut Length
Number of strips to cut
Number placement

TIP: You may need to sew smaller pieces of the same color, end to end, to enable you to cut a longer piece. This adds to the charm of the scrappy look.

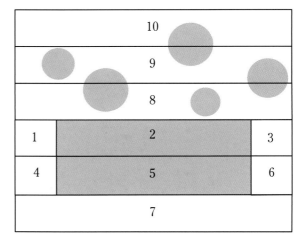

A - Flower Basket Block

1. Sew together 1st:
I - House Block
All strips are $2^1/2$" wide by the indicated length.

Color	Cut Size	# of Cuts	Position
Brown	$10^1/2$"	1	10
Brown	$14^1/2$"	1	12
Brown	$6^1/2$"	3	7, 28, 29
Brown	$4^1/2$"	5	16, 18, 22, 24, 31
Red	$14^1/2$"	4	13, 14, 20, 26
Red	$6^1/2$"	3	27, 30, 34
Red	$4^1/2$"	2	32, 33
Red	$2^1/2$"	8	2, 4, 15, 17, 19, 21, 23, 25
Ivory	$2^1/2$"	3	3, 9, 11
Ivory	$4^1/2$"	4	1, 5, 6, 8
Ivory	$14^1/2$"	1	35

It is necessary to sew units together before continuing.
Example:
Sew the rows with the windows first.
Sew the column with the window next.
Sew the chimney and roof rows.

3. Sew together 3rd
A - Flower Basket Block
All strips are $2^1/2$" wide by the indicated length.

Color	Cut Size	# of Cuts	Position
Red	$12^1/2$"	2	for Applique Circles
Brown	$10^1/2$"	2	2, 5
Ivory	$14^1/2$"	4	7, 8, 9, 10
Ivory	$2^1/2$"	4	1, 3, 4, 6

It is necessary to sew units together before continuing.
Example:
Sew the rows with basket first.

Appliqué

Sew 2 Red strips together side by side. Press.
Use the circles template on pages 10 - 11 to cut Red circles.
Applique the flower circles using the method of your choice, pg 12.
Refer to the quilt photograph for placement.

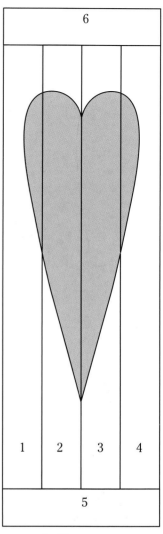

H - Pine Tree Block

2. Sew together 2nd
H - Pine Tree Block
All strips are $2^1/2$" wide by the indicated length.

Color	Cut Size	# of Cuts	Position
✓ Brown	$2^1/2$"	1	14
✓ Green	$6^1/2$"	3	10, 11, 12
✓ Green	$4^1/2$"	3	1, 6, 7
✓ Ivory	$6^1/2$"	3	3, 4, 5
✓ Ivory	$2^1/2$"	3	2, 13, 15
✓ Ivory	$1^1/2$" x $4^1/2$"	2	8, 9

It is necessary to sew units together before continuing.
Example:
    Sew the rows for the tree trunk first.
    Sew the rows for the tops of the tree.

4. Sew together 4th
C - Heart Block
All strips are $2^1/2$" wide by the indicated length.

Color	Cut Size	# of Cuts	Position
✓ Red	19"	4	for Applique Heart
✓ Ivory	$24^1/2$"	4	1, 2, 3, 4
✓ Ivory	$8^1/2$"	2	5, 6

It is necessary to sew units together before continuing.
Example:
    Sew the vertical rows side by side first.

Appliqué

Sew 4 Red strips together side by side. Press.
Use the heart pattern on pages 10 - 11 to cut Red heart.
Applique the heart using the method of your choice, pg 12.
Refer to the quilt photograph for placement.

C - Heart Block

5. Sew together 5th
D - Hourglass
All strips are $2^1/2$" wide by the indicated length.

Color	Cut Size	# of Cuts	Position
Brown	14"	3	A-half-square triangles
Ivory	14"	3	B-half-square triangles
Ivory	$10^1/2$"	2	1, 2

Sew 3 Brown strips together side by side to make a unit. Press.
Sew 3 Ivory strips together side by side to make a unit. Press.

Cut Brown unit into 2 squares $6^1/2$" x $6^1/2$".
Cut Ivory unit into 2 squares $6^1/2$" x $6^1/2$".

Construct 4 strip pieced half-square triangles (A). See page 16.

It is necessary to sew units together before continuing.
Example:
    Sew the top row of half-square triangles together first.
    Sew the bottom row of half-square triangles together next.
    Sew the top and bottom rows together.

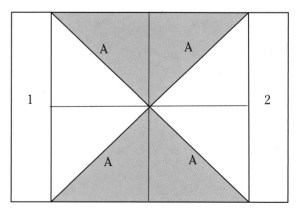

D - Hourglass

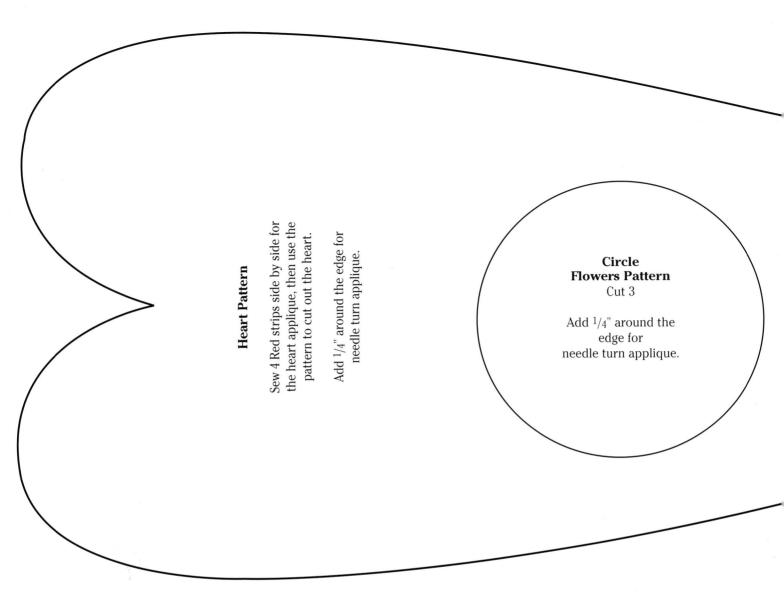

Heart Pattern

Sew 4 Red strips side by side for the heart applique, then use the pattern to cut out the heart.

Add 1/4" around the edge for needle turn applique.

**Circle
Flowers Pattern**
Cut 3

Add 1/4" around the
edge for
needle turn applique.

6. Sew together 6th
G - Windmill
All strips are $2^{1}/2$" wide by the indicated length.

Color	Cut Size	# of Cuts	Position
Brown	14"	3	A-half-square triangles
Ivory	14"	3	A-half-square triangles
Ivory	$10^{1}/2$"	2	1, 2

Sew 3 Brown strips together side by side to make a unit. Press.
Sew 3 Ivory strips together side by side to make a unit. Press.

Cut Brown unit into 2 squares $6^{1}/2$" x $6^{1}/2$".
Cut Ivory unit into 2 squares $6^{1}/2$" x $6^{1}/2$".

Construct 4 strip pieced half-square triangles (A). See page 16.

It is necessary to sew units together before continuing.
Example:
Sew the top row of half-square triangles together first.
Sew the bottom row of half-square triangles together next.
Sew the top and bottom rows together.

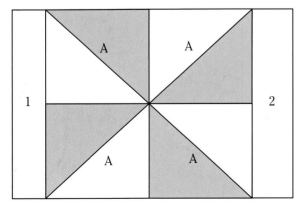

G - Windmill Block

Leaf Pattern
Cut 6
Add 1/4" around the edge for
needle turn applique.

**Circle
Flowers Pattern**
Cut 2

Add 1/4" around the
edge for
needle turn applique.

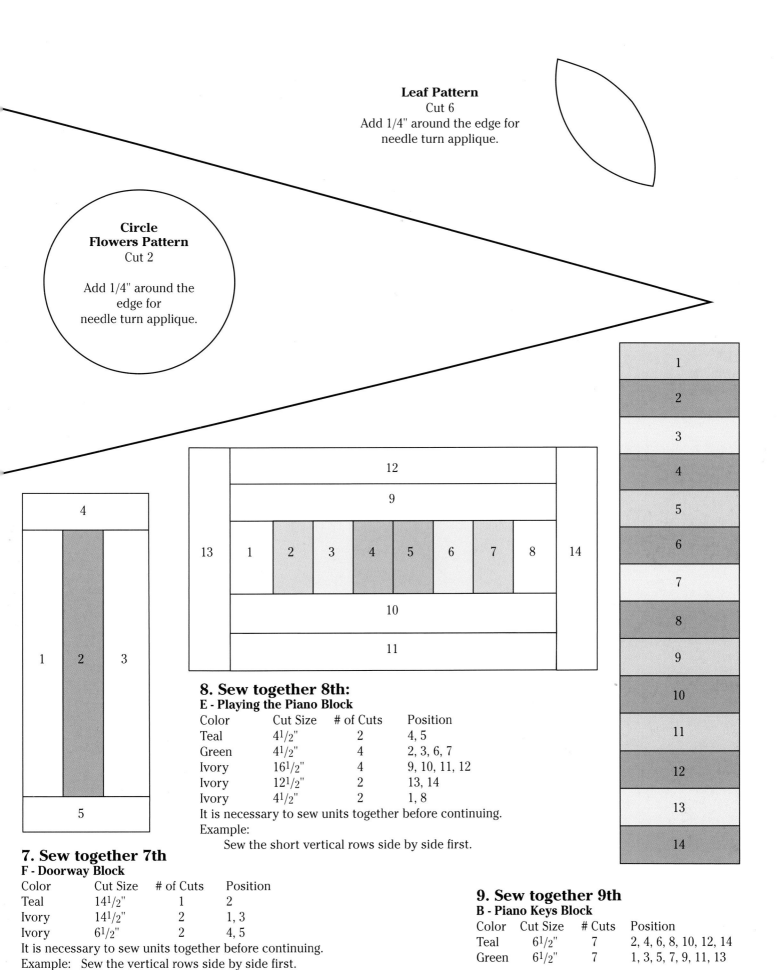

8. Sew together 8th:
E - Playing the Piano Block

Color	Cut Size	# of Cuts	Position
Teal	4 1/2"	2	4, 5
Green	4 1/2"	4	2, 3, 6, 7
Ivory	16 1/2"	4	9, 10, 11, 12
Ivory	12 1/2"	2	13, 14
Ivory	4 1/2"	2	1, 8

It is necessary to sew units together before continuing.
Example:
Sew the short vertical rows side by side first.

7. Sew together 7th
F - Doorway Block

Color	Cut Size	# of Cuts	Position
Teal	14 1/2"	1	2
Ivory	14 1/2"	2	1, 3
Ivory	6 1/2"	2	4, 5

It is necessary to sew units together before continuing.
Example: Sew the vertical rows side by side first.

9. Sew together 9th
B - Piano Keys Block

Color	Cut Size	# Cuts	Position
Teal	6 1/2"	7	2, 4, 6, 8, 10, 12, 14
Green	6 1/2"	7	1, 3, 5, 7, 9, 11, 13

Applique Instructions

Basic Turned Edge

1. Trace pattern onto template plastic.

2. Cut out the shape leaving a scant ¼" fabric border all around and clip the curves.

3. Place the template plastic on the wrong side of the fabric. Spray edges with starch.

4. Press the ⅛" border over the edge of the template plastic with the tip of a hot iron. Press firmly.

5. Remove the template, maintaining the folded edge on the back of the fabric.

6. Position the shape on the quilt and Blindstitch in place.

Basic Needle Turn

1. Cut out the shape leaving a ¼" fabric border all around.

2. Baste the shapes to the quilt, keeping the basting stitches away from the edge of the fabric.

3. Begin with all areas that are under other layers and work to the topmost layer.

4. For an area no more than 2" ahead of where you are working, trim to ⅛" and clip the curves.

5. Using the needle, roll the edge under and sew tiny Blindstitches to secure.

Using Fusible Web for Iron-on Applique:

1. Trace the pattern onto *Steam a Seam 2* fusible web.

2. Press the patterns onto the wrong side of the fabric.

3. Cut out patterns exactly on the drawn line.

4. Score the web paper with a pin, then remove the paper.

5. Position the fabric, fusible side down, on the quilt. Press with a hot iron following the fusible web manufacturer's instructions.

6. Stitch around the edge by hand.

Optional: Stabilize the wrong side of the fabric with your favorite stabilizer.

Use a size 80 machine embroidery needle. Fill the bobbin with lightweight basting thread and thread the machine with a machine embroidery thread that complements the color being appliqued.

Set your machine for a Zigzag stitch and adjust the thread tension if needed. Use a scrap to experiment with different stitch widths and lengths until you find the one you like best.

Sew slowly.

Rotary Cutting Tips

Rotary Cutter: Friend or Foe

A rotary cutter is a wonderful and useful. When not used correctly, the sharp blade can be a dangerous tool. Follow these safety tips:

1. Never cut toward you.

2. Use a sharp blade. Pressing harder on a dull blade can cause the blade to jump the ruler and injure your fingers.

3. Always disengage the blade before the cutter leaves your hand, even if you intend to pick it up immediately.

Rotary cutters have been caught when lifting fabric, have fallen onto the floor and have cut fingers.

Basic Cutting Instructions

Tips for Accurate Cutting:

Accurate cutting is easy when using a rotary cutter with a sharp blade, a cutting mat, and a transparent ruler. Begin by pressing your fabric and then follow these steps:

1. Folding:

a) Fold the fabric with the selvage edges together. Smooth the fabric flat. If needed, fold again to make your fabric length smaller than the length of the ruler.

b) Align the fold with one of the guide lines on the mat. This is important to avoid getting a kink in your strip.

2. Cutting:

a) Align the ruler with a guide line on the mat. Press down on the ruler to prevent it shifting or have someone help hold the ruler. Hold the rotary cutter along the edge of the ruler and cut off the selvage edge.

b) Also using the guide line on the mat, cut the ends straight.

c) Strips for making the quilt top may be cut on 'crosswise grain' (from selvage to selvage) or 'on grain' (parallel to the selvage edge).

Strips for borders should be cut on grain (parallel to the selvage edge) to prevent wavy edges and make quilting easier.

d) When cutting strips, move the ruler, NOT the fabric.

Basic Sewing Instructions

You now have precisely cut strips that are exactly the correct width. You are well on your way to blocks that fit together perfectly. Accurate sewing is the next important step.

Matching Edges:

1. Carefully line up the edges of your strips. Many times, if the underside is off a little, your seam will be off by $\frac{1}{8}$". This does not sound like much until you have 8 seams in a block, each off by $\frac{1}{8}$". Now your finished block is a whole inch wrong!

2. Pin the pieces together to prevent them shifting.

Seam Allowance:

I cannot stress enough the importance of accurate $\frac{1}{4}$" seams. All the quilts in this book are measured for $\frac{1}{4}$" seams unless otherwise indicated.

Most sewing machine manufacturers offer a Quarter-inch foot. A Quarter-inch foot is the most worthwhile investment you can make in your quilting.

Pressing:

I want to talk about pressing even before we get to sewing because proper pressing can make the difference between a quilt that wins a ribbon at the quilt show and one that does not.

Press, do NOT iron. What does that mean? Many of us want to move the iron back and forth along the seam. This "ironing" stretches the strip out of shape and creates errors that accumulate as the quilt is constructed. Believe it or not, there is a correct way to press your seams, and here it is:

1. Do NOT use steam with your iron. If you need a little water, spritz it on.

2. Place your fabric flat on the ironing board without opening the seam. Set a hot iron on the seam and count to 3. Lift the iron and move to the next position along the seam. Repeat until the entire seam is pressed. This sets and sinks the threads into the fabric.

3. Now, carefully lift the top strip and fold it away from you so the seam is on one side. Usually the seam is pressed toward the darker fabric, but often the direction of the seam is determined by the piecing requirements.

4. Press the seam open with your fingers. Add a little water or spray starch if it wants to close again. Lift the iron and place it on the seam. Count to 3. Lift the iron again and continue until the seam is pressed. Do NOT use the tip of the iron to push the seam open. So many people do this and wonder later why their blocks are not fitting together.

5. Most critical of all: For accuracy every seam must be pressed before the next seam is sewn.

Working with 'Crosswise Grain' strips:

Strips cut on the crosswise grain (from selvage to selvage) have problems similar to bias edges and are prone to stretching. To reduce stretching and make your quilt lay flat for quilting, keep these tips in mind.

1. Take care not to stretch the strips as you sew.

2. Adjust the sewing thread tension and the presser foot pressure if needed.

3. If you detect any puckering as you go, rip out the seam and sew it again. It is much easier to take out a seam now than to do it after the block is sewn.

Sewing Bias Edges:

Bias edges wiggle and stretch out of shape very easily. They are not recommended for beginners, but even a novice can accomplish bias edges if these techniques are employed.

1. Stabilize the bias edge with one of these methods:

    a) Press with spray starch.

    b) Press freezer paper or removable iron-on stabilizer to the back of the fabric.

    c) Sew a double row of stay stitches along the bias edge and $\frac{1}{8}$" from the bias edge. This is a favorite technique of garment makers.

2. Pin, pin, pin! I know many of us dislike pinning, but when working with bias edges, pinning makes the difference between intersections that match and those that do not.

Building Better Borders:

Wiggly borders make a quilt very difficult to finish. However, wiggly borders can be avoided with these techniques.

1. Cut the borders on grain. That means cutting your strips parallel to the selvage edge.

2. Accurately cut your borders to the exact measure of the quilt.

3. If your borders are piece stripped from crosswise grain fabrics, press well with spray starch and sew a double row of stay stitches along the outside edge to maintain the original shape and prevent stretching.

4. Pin the border to the quilt, taking care not to stretch the quilt top to make it fit. Pinning reduces slipping and stretching.

Tips for Working with Strips

TIPS: As a Guide for Yardage:
Each ¼ yard or a 'Fat Quarter' equals 3 strips
A pre-cut 'Jelly Roll' strip is 2½" x 44"
Cut 'Fat Quarter' strips to 2½" x 22"

Pre-cut strips are cut on the crosswise grain and are prone to stretching. These tips will help reduce stretching and make your quilt lay flat for quilting.

1. If you are cutting yardage, cut on the grain. Cut fat quarters on grain, parallel to the 18" side.

2. When sewing crosswise grain strips together, take care not to stretch the strips. If you detect any puckering as you go, rip out the seam and sew it again.

3. Press, Do Not Iron. Carefully open fabric, with the seam to one side, press without moving the iron. A back-and-forth ironing motion stretches the fabric.

4. Reduce the wiggle in your borders with this technique from garment making. First, accurately cut your borders to the exact measure of the quilt top. Then, before sewing the border to the quilt, run a double row of stay stitches along the outside edge to maintain the original shape and prevent stretching. Pin the border to the quilt, taking care not to stretch the quilt top to make it fit. Pinning reduces slipping and stretching.

Basic Layering Instructions

Marking Your Quilt:

If you choose to mark your quilt for hand or machine quilting, it is much easier to do so before layering. Press your quilt before you begin. Here are some handy tips regarding marking.

1. A disappearing pen may vanish before you finish.
2. Use a White pencil on dark fabrics.
3. If using a washable Blue pen, remember that pressing may make the pen permanent.

Pieced Backings:

1. Press the backing fabric before measuring.
2. If possible cut backing fabrics on grain, parallel to the selvage edges.
3. Piece 3 parts rather than 2 whenever possible, sewing 2 side borders to the center. This reduces stress on the pieced seam.
4. The backing and batting should extend at least 2" on each side of the quilt.

Creating a Quilt Sandwich:

1. Press the backing and top to remove all wrinkles.
2. Lay the backing wrong side up on the table.
3. Position the batting over the backing and smooth out all wrinkles.
4. Center the quilt top over the batting leaving a 2" border all around.
5. Pin the layers together with 2" safety pins positioned a handwidth apart. A grapefruit spoon makes inserting the pins easier. Leaving the pins open in the container speeds up the basting on the next quilt.

Basic Quilting Instructions

Hand Quilting:

Many quilters enjoy the serenity of hand quilting. Because the quilt is handled a great deal, it is important to securely baste the sandwich together. Place the quilt in a hoop and don't forget to hide your knots.

Machine Quilting:

All the quilts in this book were machine quilted. Some were quilted on a large, free-arm quilting machine and others were quilted on a sewing machine. If you have never machine quilted before, practice on some scraps first.

Straight Line Machine Quilting Tips:

1. Pin baste the layers securely.

2. Set up your sewing machine with a size 80 quilting needle and a walking foot.

3. Experimenting with the decorative stitches on your machine adds interest to your quilt. You do not have to quilt the entire piece with the same stitch. Variety is the spice of life, so have fun trying out stitches you have never used before as well as your favorite stand-bys.

Free Motion Machine Quilting Tips:

1. Pin baste the layers securely.

2. Set up your sewing machine with a spring needle, a quilting foot, and lower the feed dogs.

Basic Mitered Binding Instructions

A Perfect Finish:

The binding endures the most stress on a quilt and is usually the first thing to wear out. For this reason, we recommend using a double fold binding.

1. Trim the backing and batting even with the quilt edge.

2. If possible cut strips on the crosswise grain because a little bias in the binding is a Good thing. This is the only place in the quilt where bias is helpful, for it allows the binding to give as it is turned to the back and sewn in place.

3. Strips are usually cut 2½" wide, but check the instructions for your project before cutting.

4. Sew strips end to end to make a long strip sufficient to go all around the quilt plus 4"- 6".

5. With wrong sides together, fold the strip in half lengthwise. Press.

6. Stretch out your hand and place your little finger at the corner of the quilt top. Place the binding where your thumb touches the edge of the quilt. Aligning the edge of the quilt with the raw edges of the binding, pin the binding in place along the first side.

7. Leaving a 2" tail for later use, begin sewing the binding to the quilt with a ¼" seam.

For Mitered Corners:

1. Stop ¼" from the first corner. Leave the needle in the quilt and turn it 90°. Hit the reverse button on your machine and back off the quilt leaving the threads connected.

2. Fold the binding perpendicular to the side you sewed, making a 45° angle. Carefully maintaining the first fold, bring the binding back along the edge to be sewn.

3. Carefully align the edges of the binding with the quilt edge and sew as you did the first side. Repeat this process until you reach the tail left at the beginning. Fold the tail out of the way and sew until you are ¼" from the beginning stitches.

4. Remove the quilt from the machine. Fold the quilt out of the way and match the binding tails together. Carefully sew the binding tails with a ¼" seam. You can do this by hand if you prefer.

Finishing the Binding:

5. Trim the seam to reduce bulk.

6. Finish stitching the binding to the quilt across the join you just sewed.

7. Turn the binding to the back of the quilt. To reduce bulk at the corners, fold the miter in the opposite direction from which it was folded on the front.

8. Hand-sew a Blind stitch on the back of the quilt to secure the binding in place.

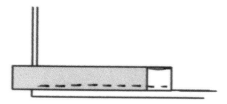

Align the raw edge of the binding with the raw edge of the quilt top. Start about 8" from the corner and go along the first side with a ¼" seam.

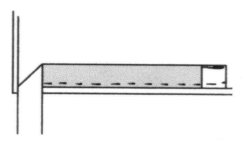

Stop ¼" from the edge. Then stitch a slant to the corner (through both layers of binding)... lift up, then down, as you line up the edge. Fold the binding back.

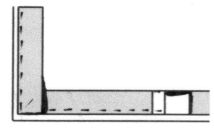

Align the raw edge again. Continue stitching the next side with a ¼" seam as you sew the binding in place.

Half-Square Triangles

Sew 3 Brown strips side by side.

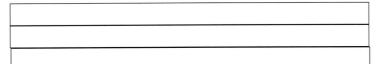

Sew 3 Ivory strips side by side.

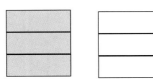

Cut
Brown unit
into 2
squares
$6^{1}/_{2}$" x $6^{1}/_{2}$".

Cut
Ivory unit
into 2
squares
$6^{1}/_{2}$" x $6^{1}/_{2}$".

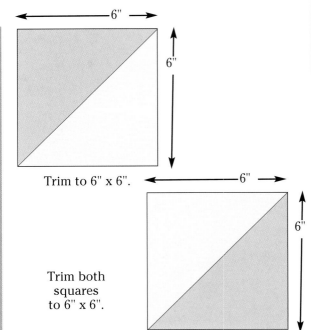

Trim to 6" x 6".

Trim both
squares
to 6" x 6".

Trim to 6" x 6".

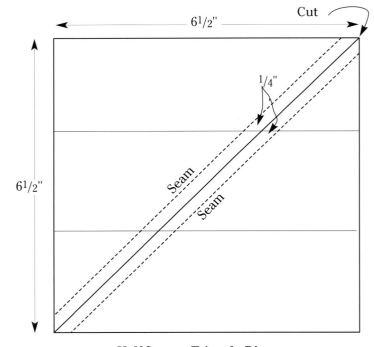

Half-Square Triangle Diagram

1. Place 2 squares right side together.
2. Draw a diagonal line from corner to corner.
3. Stitch $^{1}/_{4}$" on each side of the line.
4. Cut squares apart on the diagonal line.
5. Open the 2 new squares with 2 colors.
6. Press. Trim off dog-ears.
7. Trim to $5^{1}/_{2}$" x $5^{1}/_{2}$".

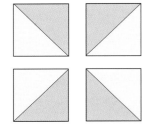

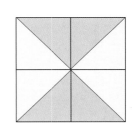

Tilt and turn 4
squares to form an
hourglass shape.
Sew squares together.

Hourglass

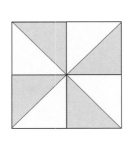

Tilt and turn 4
squares to form a
windmill shape.
Sew squares together.

Windmill

Vintage Holiday

SIZE: 54" x 70"

Yardage

We used a *Moda* "Vintage Holiday" by April Cornell
'Jelly Roll' collection of $2^1/2$" fabric strips
- we purchased 1 'Jelly Roll'

$3/4$ yard Brown	OR	8 strips
$3/4$ yard Red	OR	8 strips
$1/2$ yard Dark Green	OR	4 strips
$3/4$ yard Medium Green	OR	8 strips
1 yard Tan	OR	12 strips

Border #3   Purchase $3/4$ yard Black
Outer Border &
  Binding   Purchase $1^3/4$ yards Red
Backing   Purchase 4 yards
Batting   Purchase 76" x 60"
Sewing machine, needle, thread

Make and Sew the Blocks

Caution:
  Cut carefully.
  You will use ALL the strips.
  Cut the longest strips first.
See details for blocks on pages 6 - 11.

Preparation for Blocks

TIP: To avoid confusion, gather the strips for each block
     as you cut them and label by piece number.

All strips are $2^1/2$" wide by the indicated length.

Cutting Lists and Charts

The chart for each color includes:
  Cut Length
  Number of strips to cut
  Number placement

TIP: You may need to sew smaller pieces of the same color,
end to end, to enable you to cut a longer piece. This adds
to the charm of the scrappy look.

continued on page 18

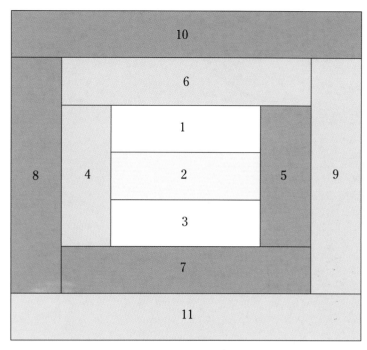

Vintage Holiday Block
Make 6

Basic Block:

Make 6 basic blocks.
You'll need Red, Green and Light Tan print strips.
All strips are $2^1/2$" wide by the indicated length.

Color	Cut Size	# of Cuts	Position
Green	$6^1/2$"	6	#4
Green	$10^1/2$"	12	#6, #9
Green	$14^1/2$"	6	#11
Red	$6^1/2$"	6	#5
Red	$10^1/2$"	12	#7, #8
Red	$14^1/2$"	6	#10

This will give you all the pieces you need to make 6 blocks

TIP: To insure a scrappy look, arrange the pieces on the table
     with assorted fabrics in each block.

SEW BLOCKS

Center of Block:

Choose 3 Tan strips, one with a definite floral print.
Sew strips together side by side, with floral strip in the center.
     to make a $6^1/2$" x 44" piece
Cut strip set into 6 units of $6^1/2$" x $6^1/2$" squares.

Finish the Block:

For each block, sew strips together in numerical sequence,
     pressing after each joining seam.
     1/2/3 to 4. Press
     1/2/3/4 to 5. Press
     1/2/3/4/5 to 6. Press
     - and so on until the block in complete.

Each block will measure $14^1/2$" x $14^1/2$".

continued from page 17

Vintage Holiday - Quilt Assembly

Suzanne McNeill

"I love designing with fabrics. The colors, feel and textures are exciting. Quilts are my favorite!"

Suzanne shares her creativity and enthusiasm in books by Design Originals. Her mission is to publish books that help others learn about the newest techniques, the best projects and popular products.

MANY THANKS to my staff for their cheerful help and wonderful ideas!
Kathy Mason • Donna Kinsey • Patty Williams
Janet Long • David & Donna Thomason
Jennifer Lokey for skillfully and patiently editing the patterns in this book

Supplier - Most quilt and fabric stores carry an excellent assortment of supplies. If you need something special, ask your local store to contact the following companies.
FABRICS, 'JELLY ROLLS', 'FAT QUARTERS'
  Moda and United Notions, Dallas, TX, 972-484-8901
QUILTERS
  Susan Corbett, 817-361-7762
  Julie Lawson, 817-428-5929
  Sue Needle, 817-589-1168

Cut Sashing
Sashing:
  You'll need 9 Dark Green strips. From each strip, cut 2 sashing strips 2^1/$_2$" x 14^1/$_2$", a total of 17 strip

Corners:
  Cut 12 corner squares 2^1/$_2$" x 2^1/$_2$"

Assembly
Arrange the 6 blocks, 14 sashing strips and 12 corner squares following the quilt diagram.

Sew each row of corner, sashing, corner, sashing and corner strips together.
  Press seams toward sashing. Make 4 rows.

Sew each row of sashing and blocks together.
  Press seams toward sashing.

Sew all rows together. Press.

Borders
Tan Pieced Border #1:
You'll need 6 different Tan print strips.
From each Tan strip, cut random lengths, no longer tha 14".
  Sew all strips together end to end.

Cut 2 strips 2^1/$_2$" x 50^1/$_2$" for sides.
Cut 2 strips 2^1/$_2$" x 38^1/$_2$" for top and bottom.
Sew the side borders to the quilt. Press.
Sew the top and bottom borders. Press.

Multi Color Border #2:
You'll need 6 different Dark Greens, Browns and Reds.
From each strip, cut random lengths, no longer than 14
  Sew all strips together end to end.

Cut 2 strips 2^1/$_2$" x 54^1/$_2$" for sides.
Cut 2 strips 2^1/$_2$" x 42^1/$_2$" for top and bottom.
Sew the side borders to the quilt. Press.
Sew the top and bottom borders. Press.

Black Border #3:
You'll need 6 Black 1^1/$_2$" strips.
  Sew all strips together end to end.

Cut 2 strips 1^1/$_2$" x 58^1/$_2$" for sides.
Cut 2 strips 1^1/$_2$" x 44^1/$_2$" for top and bottom.
Sew the side borders to the quilt. Press.
Sew the top and bottom borders. Press.

Red Print Border #4:
Cut 2 strips 5^1/$_2$" x 60^1/$_2$" for sides
Cut 2 strips 5^1/$_2$" x 54^1/$_2$" for top and bottom
Sew the side borders to the quilt. Press.
Sew the top and bottom borders. Press.

Finishing
Quilting:
  See Basic Instructions on pages 12 - 14.
Binding:
  Gather leftover strips, pieced strips and scraps of strips.
  Sew together end to end to equal 260".
  See Basic Instructions on page 15.